GIFTS
from the
Holiday Kitchen

PUBLICATIONS INTERNATIONAL, LTD.

Favorite All Time Recipes is a trademark of Publications International, Ltd.

Recipe Development: Pamela Eimers, Karen Levin

Photography: Sacco Productions Limited, Chicago

Pictured on the front cover *(clockwise from top right):* Praline Pecans & Cranberries *(page 36)*, Cherry, Almond & Chocolate Breakfast Wreath *(page 46)* and Truffles *(page 69)*.

Pictured on the back cover *(clockwise from top left):* Bon Appetito! gift basket *(pages 20–33)*, Bread Lovers' Basket gift basket *(pages 42–51)*, "Mail Order" Cookies gift basket *(pages 82–92)* and Breakfast in Bed gift basket *(pages 72–81)*.

ISBN: 0-7853-2003-2

Manufactured in U.S.A.

8   7   6   5   4   3   2   1

CONTENTS

GIFT–GIVING TIPS

Unwrapping a homemade present in beautiful packaging is one of the holiday's greatest pleasures. *Gifts from the Holiday Kitchen* makes creating these special hand-crafted gifts easier than ever before. Each recipe has detailed preparation steps and full-color photographs illustrating innovative packaging ideas for a variety of gifts, including gift baskets. Delight your family and friends by giving the most meaningful gift of all—one crafted by hand that's from the heart.

THE PERFECT PACKAGE

Homemade gifts are made extraordinary when tucked into unique packages lavished with decorative accessories. Craft, stationary and kitchen supply stores carry a wide variety of supplies that can add a special touch to your gifts.

Airtight Canisters: These containers are available in a variety of materials, including glass and plastic, and are essential for gifts that must be securely packed. They are also great for scone and pancake mixes and storing snack mixes, cookies and peanut brittles.

Baskets: These versatile holdalls are available in a wide variety of materials and sizes. Large, sturdy ones are well suited for packing entire gift themes. Oblong shapes are wonderful for breads and smaller versions are just right for cookies and brownies.

Bottles: Assorted airtight bottles etched with decorative patterns are perfect for flavored vinegars, salad dressings and syrups. Always choose securely stoppered bottles to help prevent any leakage.

Boxes: Boxes come in a variety of shapes and sizes and are well suited for cookies, candies, snack mixes, crackers and truffles. Large boxes are perfect for packing entire gift themes.

Gift Bags: These handy totes come in a variety of shapes and sizes. Pack individual brownies and truffles in smaller bags, and goodie-filled bottles, jars and canisters in larger bags.

Glass Jars: Jars are perfect for packing pestos, flavored butters and snack mixes. Be sure to pack more perishable items, such as sauces, chutneys and spreads in jars with airtight lids.

Packing Peanuts and Bubble Wrap: When shipping your baskets these items are essential. Wrapping all breakable containers in bubble wrap and filling boxes with packing peanuts will help avoid damage during shipping.

Pails: Plastic and metal pails are the right choice for holding smaller items such as snack mixes, cookies

Clockwise from top right: Baskets, Canisters, Jars, Packing Peanuts, Gift Bags, Pails, Tins, Boxes and Bottles.

and candies. Colorful plastic pails are also wonderful holdalls for children's gifts.

Tins: Metal containers with tight-fitting lids are just the thing for brittles, snack mixes, breads, candies and truffles, and they hold up well when sent through the mail. Lidded molds and bread pans are also great for stacked cookies, brownies or truffles.

THE FINISHING TOUCHES

After the goodies are made and tucked into decorative packages, you are ready to put the finishing touches on your gift.

Cellophane: An indispensable material for hard-to-wrap gifts such as plates of food, individual breads, candies and pies. Gather the ends and secure with satiny ribbons for a pretty finish.

Decorative Papers: Wrapping papers come in a variety of finishes, including glossy and metallic, and many can be enhanced with rubber stamps. Colorful tissue papers are perfect for tucking into gift boxes, bags and pails and are a good substitute for wrapping paper. Or, for a variation on gift wrapping, try gluing paper onto boxes and lids and secure the covered boxes with cords or strings.

Gift Tags: Assorted foil and paper tags come in handy when making personalized notes and cards for your gifts. They also make great labels for storing directions.

Raffia: Tuck assorted colors of raffia into boxes, baskets and pails. Or, use it as ribbon and tie boxes and tins with pretty bows.

Ribbons, Satin Cords and Strings: Thick, colorful ribbons, metallic strings and thin, shiny cords are perfect accents for homemade wrapping papers. Make packages more whimsical by tying them with a rainbow of ribbons. Or, spruce up durable cookies by stacking and tying them together with a cord or metallic string.

Rubber Stamps and Ink Pads: Stamps with holiday or food themes paired with colorful inks are perfect for decorating plain papers for wrapping and making personalized note cards for recipes, labels for sauces and pestos, storing directions, and gift tags.

SPECIAL INSTRUCTIONS

Before you give your gifts, did you remember to include:

Storage directions? They are included at the end of every recipe and it's a good idea to include them with your gifts. Storage directions are an absolute must for perishable items and those that must be held in the refrigerator.

Serving notes and suggestions? Valuable serving tips are included at the end of some of the recipes, and many photographs illustrate innovative serving suggestions and uses for your edible gifts.

Recipes and subrecipes? Several gifts, such as the mixes, provide the base for other recipes. By including those recipes with your package, you'll take the guesswork out of preparation for your presents.

Clockwise from top right: Tissue Papers, Decorative Papers, Raffia, Rubber Stamps and Ink Pads, Gift Tags, Ribbons and Cellophane.

Caramel-Pecan Thumbprint Cookies

2 cups pecan
    halves or pieces
2 eggs
1 cup butter or
    margarine,
    softened
    (page 74)
⅔ cup packed brown
    sugar
1 teaspoon vanilla
2¼ cups all-purpose
    flour
    Caramel Filling
    (page 10)
    Chocolate
    sprinkles

1. Preheat oven to 375°F. Place pecans in work bowl of food processor; process using on/off pulsing action until evenly chopped. Place nuts in medium bowl. Set aside.

2. To separate egg white from yolk, gently tap egg in center against hard surface, such as side of bowl. Holding shell half in each hand, gently transfer yolk back and forth between 2 shell halves. Allow white to drip down between 2 shells into bowl.

3. When all white has dripped into bowl, place yolk in another bowl. (Transfer white to third bowl. Repeat with remaining egg.)

4. Beat butter and sugar in large bowl with electric mixer at medium speed until light and fluffy. Beat in egg yolks and vanilla until well blended, scraping down side of bowl occasionally. Beat in flour at low speed until soft dough forms, scraping down side of bowl once.

5. Shape 2 level teaspoons dough into 1-inch ball with lightly floured hands. Place ball on waxed paper. Repeat with remaining dough.

continued on page 10

Caramel-Pecan Thumbprint Cookies, continued

6. Dip balls, one at a time, into egg whites, turning with spoon to coat completely. Remove balls with fork, letting excess egg whites drip back into bowl. Roll balls in nuts to coat, pressing nuts gently into dough with fingers.

7. Place cookies 1 inch apart on *ungreased* baking sheets. Press thumb firmly into center of each cookie.

8. Bake 10 to 12 minutes or until golden brown. Quickly repress thumbprints with thumb or end of wooden spoon. Remove cookies with spatula to wire racks. Cool completely.

9. Prepare Caramel Filling. Spoon ¼ to ½ teaspoon filling into each thumbprint. Sprinkle chocolate sprinkles over fillings. Let stand 2 hours or until set.

10. Store tightly covered in refrigerator up to 1 week.

Makes 4 dozen cookies

Caramel Filling

½ **cup sugar**
¼ **teaspoon lemon juice**
¼ **cup whipping cream**

1. Combine sugar and lemon juice in small saucepan. Heat over medium-high heat 6 to 8 minutes or until sugar melts and is light caramel color, stirring constantly with wooden spoon.

2. Add cream. Bring to a boil over medium-high heat; boil 1 minute, stirring constantly. Pour into nonplastic bowl. Let stand 20 to 30 minutes or until thick but not sticky.

Makes about ½ cup

Walnut Tartlets with Chocolate Ganache Filling

Chocolate Leaves (page 12)
½ cup walnut halves
1 cup all-purpose flour
¼ cup sugar
1 tablespoon grated lemon peel (page 49)
⅓ cup butter or margarine, cut into pieces
1 egg, slightly beaten
Chocolate Ganache (page 12)

1. Prepare Chocolate Leaves. Set aside.

2. Preheat oven to 350°F. To toast walnuts, spread walnuts in single layer in baking pan. Bake 8 to 12 minutes or until browned, stirring frequently with wooden spoon.

3. Place walnuts in work bowl of food processor. Process using on/off pulsing action until walnuts are finely chopped, but not pasty.

4. Reserve 2 tablespoons walnuts. Place remaining walnuts in medium bowl. Add flour, sugar and lemon peel; blend well. Cut in butter with pastry blender or two knives until mixture resembles coarse crumbs. Stir in egg with fork until mixture holds together.

5. Spoon 2 teaspoonfuls mixture into *ungreased* mini-muffin cups. Press dough onto bottom and up side of each cup with fingers.

6. Bake 16 to 20 minutes or until golden brown. Cool 5 minutes in pan. Remove shells from pans. Cool completely on wire racks.

7. Prepare Chocolate Ganache. Spoon ½ teaspoon ganache into each shell. Sprinkle reserved 2 tablespoons chopped nuts evenly over shells. Gently push chocolate leaf into each shell.

8. Store tightly covered in refrigerator up to 1 week.

Makes 30 tartlets

continued on page 12

Walnut Tartlets with Chocolate Ganache Filling, continued

Chocolate Leaves

Assorted nontoxic fresh leaves such as rose, lemon or camellia*

½ cup (2 ounces) chopped semisweet chocolate or semisweet chocolate chips

1 teaspoon shortening

EQUIPMENT:

Paint brush or pastry brush

*Nontoxic leaves are available in florist shops.

1. Wash leaves; pat dry with paper towels. Set aside. Place large sheet heavy-duty foil on counter.

2. Fill saucepan ¼ full (about 1 inch deep) with warm water. Place chocolate and shortening in 1-cup glass measure. To melt chocolate, place measure in warm water; stir frequently with rubber spatula until smooth. (Be careful not to get any water into chocolate or chocolate may become lumpy.)

3. Brush melted chocolate onto underside of each leaf with paint brush or pastry brush, coating leaf thickly and evenly.

4. Carefully wipe off any chocolate that may have run onto front of leaf.

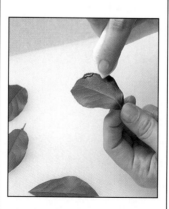

5. Place leaves, chocolate-sides up, on foil. Let stand 1 hour or until chocolate is set.

6. Carefully peel leaves away from chocolate beginning at stem ends; refrigerate chocolate leaves until ready to use.

Makes 30 to 40 leaves

Chocolate Ganache

2 tablespoons whipping cream

1 tablespoon butter

½ cup (2 ounces) chopped semisweet chocolate or semisweet chocolate chips

½ teaspoon vanilla

Heat whipping cream and butter in small saucepan over medium heat until butter melts and mixture boils, stirring frequently with wooden spoon. Remove saucepan from heat. Stir in chocolate and vanilla until mixture is smooth, returning to heat for 20 to 30 second intervals as needed to melt chocolate. Keep warm (ganache is semi-firm at room temperature).

Makes about ½ cup

Sugar Cookies

1 cup sugar
1 cup butter or margarine
2 eggs
½ teaspoon lemon extract
½ teaspoon vanilla
3 cups all-purpose flour
1 teaspoon baking powder
¼ teaspoon salt
  Egg Yolk Paint (page 16)
  Royal Icing (page 92)
  Decorator Frosting (page 16)
EQUIPMENT AND DECORATIONS:
  Liquid or paste food coloring
  Small paint brushes
  Sponges

1. Beat sugar and butter in large bowl with electric mixer at medium speed until light and fluffy. Beat in eggs and extracts at medium speed until well blended, scraping down side of bowl occasionally (mixture will look grainy). Beat in 1 cup flour, baking powder and salt at medium speed until well blended. Gradually add remaining 2 cups flour. Beat at low speed until soft dough forms, scraping down side of bowl once.

2. Form dough into 3 discs. Wrap discs in plastic wrap; refrigerate 2 hours or until dough is firm.

3. Preheat oven to 375°F. Working with 1 disc at a time, unwrap dough and place on lightly floured surface. Roll out dough with lightly floured rolling pin to ⅛-inch thickness.

4. Cut dough with lightly floured 3- to 4-inch cookie cutters. Place cutouts 1 inch apart on *ungreased* cookie sheets. Gently press dough trimmings together; reroll and cut out more cookies. (If dough is sticky, pat into disc; wrap in plastic wrap and refrigerate until firm before rerolling.)

5. To paint cookies before baking, prepare Egg Yolk Paint. Divide paint among several bowls; tint with liquid food coloring, if desired.

6. Paint yolk paint onto unbaked cookies with paint brush.

7. Bake 7 to 9 minutes or until cookies are set. Remove cookies with spatula to wire rack; cool completely.

continued on page 16

Sugar Cookies, continued

8. To sponge paint cooled cookies, prepare Royal Icing. Divide icing among several bowls; tint with liquid or paste food coloring. For best results, use 2 to 3 shades of the same color. (If icing is too thick, stir in water, 1 drop at a time, with spoon until spreadable consistency.)

9. Spread thin layer of icing on cookies to within ⅛ inch of edges with small spatula. Let stand 30 minutes at room temperature or until icing is set.

10. Cut clean kitchen sponge into 1-inch squares with scissors. Dip sponge into tinted icing, scraping against side of bowl to remove excess icing. Gently press sponge on base icing several times until desired effect is achieved. Let stand 15 minutes or until icing is set.

11. To pipe additional decorations on cookies, prepare Decorator Frosting. Tint frosting as directed in Step 8, if desired.

12. Place each color frosting in piping bag fitted with small writing tip or resealable plastic freezer bags with one small corner cut off. Decorate as desired. Let cookies stand at room temperature until piping is set.

13. Store loosely covered at room temperature up to 1 week.

Makes about 3 dozen cookies

Egg Yolk Paint

2 egg yolks (page 8)
2 teaspoons water

Combine egg yolks and water in small bowl with fork until blended.

Makes about ⅓ cup

Note: Only brush this paint onto unbaked cookies.

Decorator Frosting

¾ cup butter, softened (page 74)
4½ cups powdered sugar, sifted
3 tablespoons water
1 teaspoon vanilla
¼ teaspoon lemon extract

Beat butter in medium bowl with electric mixer at medium speed until smooth. Add 2 cups sugar. Beat at medium speed until light and fluffy. Add water and extracts. Beat at low speed until well blended, scraping down side of bowl once. Beat in remaining 2½ cups sugar until mixture is creamy.

Makes 2 cups

Note: This frosting is perfect for piping, but is less durable than Royal Icing. Bumping, stacking and handling may damage decorations.

Candy Cane & Wreath Ornaments

1 cup sugar
½ cup shortening
½ cup butter or
    margarine
1 teaspoon salt
1 egg
2 teaspoons vanilla
2½ cups all-purpose
    flour
½ teaspoon almond
    extract
¼ teaspoon liquid
    green food
    coloring
¼ teaspoon
    peppermint
    extract
½ teaspoon liquid
    red food
    coloring,
    divided
**Decorator
    Frosting
    (page 16)**
**EQUIPMENT AND
    DECORATIONS:**
**Assorted red
    candies
Ribbon**

1. Beat sugar, shortening, butter and salt in large bowl with electric mixer at medium speed until light and fluffy, scraping down side of bowl once. Beat in egg and vanilla until well blended. Beat in flour at low speed until soft dough forms, scraping down side of bowl once.

2. Remove half of dough from bowl. Set aside. Divide remaining dough evenly between 2 medium bowls. Stir almond extract and green food coloring into one portion with wooden spoon until well blended.

3. Stir peppermint extract and ¼ teaspoon red food coloring into remaining portion until well blended.

4. Place level teaspoonfuls of each dough on large baking sheet. Cover; refrigerate 15 minutes or until slightly firm.

5. Preheat oven to 375°F. Place 1 teaspoon red dough, 1 teaspoon green dough and 2 teaspoons uncolored dough on lightly floured surface. Roll out each portion into 6- to 7-inch rope with lightly floured hands.

6. Place 1 green rope next to 1 uncolored rope and 1 red rope next to remaining uncolored rope. Twist each pair of ropes together 7 or 8 times; place on *ungreased* baking sheet.

continued on page 18

Candy Cane & Wreath Ornaments, continued

7. Shape red and white rope into candy cane and green and white rope into wreath. Repeat with remaining dough.

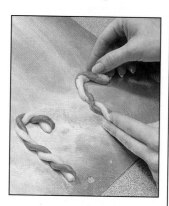

8. Bake 7 to 9 minutes or until cookies are firm. *Do not allow to brown.* Transfer cookies with spatula to wire racks; cool completely.

9. Prepare Decorator Frosting. Tint half of frosting with remaining ¼ teaspoon red liquid food coloring. Spoon frostings into piping bags fitted with writing tips.

10. Pipe cluster of berries onto wreaths with red frosting. Glue candies onto wreaths with white frosting. Let stand 1 hour or until icing is set. Tie ribbon loops or bows onto each cookie for hanging.

Makes about 4 dozen cookies

Mocha Espresso

2 tablespoons
    Mocha
    Espresso Mix
    (recipe follows)
6 ounces boiling
    water
    Whipping cream,
    whipped
    (optional)

Spoon 2 tablespoons espresso mix into cup or mug. Add 6 ounces boiling water; stir. Serve with whipping cream, if desired.

Makes 1 serving

Mocha Espresso Mix

4 ounces semisweet
    chocolate
    (squares or
    bars)
¾ cup nonfat dry
    milk powder
½ cup espresso
    powder
½ teaspoon ground
    cinnamon

1. Place chocolate on cutting board; shave into small pieces with paring knife.

2. Combine chocolate, dry milk powder, espresso powder and cinnamon in small bowl until well blended.

3. Spoon mixture into clean, dry decorative glass jar with tight-fitting lid; cover.

4. Store in airtight container at room temperature up to 1 month.

Makes about 1⅔ cups

Sun-Dried Tomato Pesto

1 tablespoon
    vegetable oil
½ cup pine nuts
2 cloves garlic
1 bunch Italian
    parsley
⅛ pound Parmesan
    cheese
1 jar (8 ounces)
    sun-dried
    tomatoes
    packed in oil,
    undrained
¼ cup coarsely
    chopped pitted
    calamata olives
2 teaspoons dried
    basil leaves
¼ teaspoon crushed
    red pepper

1. To toast pine nuts, heat oil in small skillet over medium-low heat. Add pine nuts; cook 30 to 45 seconds or until lightly browned, shaking pan constantly.

2. Remove nuts from skillet with slotted spoon; drain on paper towels.

3. To peel garlic, trim ends of garlic cloves. Slightly crush cloves, one at a time, under flat side of chef's knife blade; peel away skins. Set aside.

4. To remove stems from parsley, strip leaves from stems with hands. Pack parsley leaves into measuring cup to equal 1 cup. Set aside.

5. Grate Parmesan cheese using bell grater or hand-held grater. Measure ½ cup. Set aside.

6. Combine pine nuts and garlic in work bowl of food processor. Process using on/off pulsing action until mixture is finely chopped.

7. Add undrained tomatoes to work bowl; process until finely chopped. Add parsley, cheese, olives, basil and pepper; process until mixture resembles thick paste, scraping down side of bowl occasionally with small spatula.

8. Spoon pesto into clean, dry decorative crock or jar with tight-fitting lid; cover.

9. Store in airtight container in refrigerator up to 1 month.

   Makes about 1½ cups

Rio Grande Salsa

1 bunch fresh
   cilantro leaves
1 canned chipotle
   chili pepper, 1
   teaspoon adobo
   sauce reserved*
1 tablespoon
   vegetable oil
1 onion, chopped
3 cloves garlic,
   minced
   (page 30)
2 teaspoons ground
   cumin
1½ teaspoons chili
   powder
2 cans (14½ ounces
   each) diced
   tomatoes,
   drained
¾ teaspoon sugar
½ teaspoon salt

*Chipotle chili peppers
are smoked jalapeño
peppers and are
commonly available
canned in adobo sauce.

1. To chop cilantro,
place cilantro in
1-cup measuring cup.
Snip enough cilantro
with kitchen scissors to
measure ½ cup. Set
aside.

2. To seed chipotle
chili, slit chili open
lengthwise with
scissors or knife.
Carefully pull out and
discard seeds and
veins. Cut into slices.

3. Holding slices
together with
fingers, finely chop with
utility knife. (Chipotle
chili peppers can sting
and irritate the skin;
wear rubber gloves
when handling peppers
and do not touch eyes.
Wash hands after
handling chili peppers.)

4. Heat oil in medium
saucepan over
medium-high heat until
hot. Add onion and
garlic. Cook and stir 5
minutes or until onion is
tender. Add cumin and
chili powder; cook 30
seconds, stirring
frequently. Add chili with
adobo sauce and
tomatoes. Reduce heat
to medium-low. Simmer
10 to 12 minutes or
until salsa is thickened,
stirring occasionally.

5. Remove saucepan
from heat; stir in
cilantro, sugar and salt.
Cool completely.

6. Store in airtight
container in
refrigerator up to
3 weeks.

Makes about 3 cups

Note: This salsa is very
spicy. For a milder
version, use 1 teaspoon
chopped chipotle chili
pepper.

Best Ever Hero Sandwiches

1 large tomato
4 (6-inch) hoagie
    rolls or Kaiser
    rolls
¼ cup Hot & Spicy
    Mustard (recipe
    follows)
4 ounces sliced
    salami
4 ounces sliced
    smoked ham
4 ounces sliced
    provolone
    cheese
4 large romaine
    lettuce leaves

1. To prepare tomato, trim off cap and stem end. Cut tomato into 8 slices with paring knife.

2. Split rolls lengthwise in half with chef's knife. Spread mustard evenly over bottom half of each roll.

3. Layer salami, ham, cheese, tomato and lettuce evenly on bottom half of each roll; top with top halves of rolls.

Makes 4 servings

Hot & Spicy Mustard

¼ cup whole yellow
    mustard seeds
¼ cup honey
3 tablespoons cider
    vinegar
2 tablespoons
    ground mustard
1 teaspoon salt
⅛ teaspoon ground
    cloves

1. Place ¼ cup water in small saucepan. Bring to a boil over high heat. Add mustard seeds. Cover saucepan; remove from heat. Let stand 1 hour or until liquid is absorbed.

2. Spoon mustard seeds into work bowl of food processor.

3. Add honey, vinegar, ground mustard, salt and cloves to work bowl; process using on/off pulsing action until mixture is thickened and seeds are coarsely chopped, scraping down side of work bowl once with spatula. Refrigerate at least 1 day before serving.

4. Store in airtight container in refrigerator up to 3 weeks.

Makes about 1 cup

Roasted Vegetable Tomato Sauce

1 eggplant
1½ teaspoons salt,
   divided
2 zucchini
2 red or yellow bell
   peppers
3 to 4 cloves garlic
8 ounces small
   mushrooms,
   stems trimmed
1 red onion, cut into
   ¾-inch pieces
¼ cup olive oil
2 tablespoons
   balsamic
   vinegar
1 teaspoon dried
   rosemary
1 can (28 ounces)
   tomato sauce
2 teaspoons sugar
2 teaspoons dried
   basil leaves
½ teaspoon crushed
   red pepper

1. To prepare eggplant, trim off cap and stem with chef's knife. Cut eggplant lengthwise into ¾-inch-thick slices. Place slices in large colander set over bowl; sprinkle with 1 teaspoon salt. Drain 30 minutes.

2. Rinse eggplant under cold running water. Pat dry with paper towels. Cut each slice in half with chef's knife. Holding slices together with fingers, cut crosswise into ¾-inch pieces. Set aside.

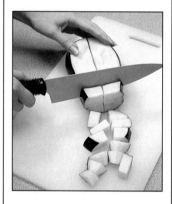

3. Scrub zucchini with vegetable brush under cold running water. Slice lengthwise into halves with utility knife. Holding halves together with fingers, cut crosswise into ½-inch pieces. Set aside.

4. Rinse bell peppers under cold running water. To seed peppers, stand on end on cutting board. Cut off sides in 3 to 4 lengthwise slices with utility knife. (Cut close to, but not through, stem.) Discard stems and seeds. Scrape out any remaining seeds.

5. Rinse insides of peppers under cold running water. Cut each slice into strips with utility knife. Cut strips into ¾-inch pieces. Set aside.

continued on page 30

Roasted Vegetable Tomato Sauce, continued

6. To mince garlic, trim ends of garlic cloves. Slightly crush cloves, one at a time, under flat side of chef's knife blade; peel away skins. Chop garlic with chef's knife until garlic is in uniform fine pieces. Set aside.

7. Preheat oven to 425°F. Combine eggplant, zucchini, bell peppers, mushrooms and onion in 15×10-inch jelly-roll pan.

8. Whisk oil, vinegar, garlic and rosemary in small bowl with wire whisk until well blended; pour over vegetables, stirring with wooden spoon until evenly coated.

9. Bake 25 minutes or until vegetables are brown and tender, stirring occasionally with wooden spoon. Sprinkle remaining ½ teaspoon salt evenly over vegetables.

10. Meanwhile, combine tomato sauce, ¾ cup water, sugar, basil and red pepper in large saucepan. Bring to a boil over high heat. Reduce heat to medium-low; cover. Simmer 10 minutes, stirring occasionally.

11. Add roasted vegetables and cooking liquid to saucepan. Cover; simmer 5 minutes, stirring occasionally. Remove saucepan from heat; cool completely.

12. Store in airtight container in refrigerator up to 5 days.

Makes about 8 cups

Italian Salad Dressing

½ **cup extra virgin olive oil**

¼ **cup Basil-Garlic Champagne Vinegar (recipe follows)**

1 **teaspoon Dijon mustard**

½ **teaspoon salt**

½ **teaspoon sugar**

¼ **teaspoon ground black pepper**

1. Whisk oil, Basil-Garlic Champagne Vinegar, mustard, salt, sugar and pepper in small bowl with wire whisk until well blended.

2. Place neck of funnel in clean, dry decorative bottle. Line funnel with double layer of cheesecloth or coffee filter.

3. Pour mixture into funnel; discard solids. Seal bottle. Store in refrigerator up to 1 month.

Makes about ¾ cup

Basil-Garlic Champagne Vinegar

1 **bunch basil leaves**

4 **cloves garlic**

4 **dried hot red peppers**

1¼ **cups champagne sherry or aged sherry vinegar**

1. Separate basil into leaves. Wash in cold water. Repeat several times to remove sand and grit. Pat dry with paper towels.

2. To separate stems from basil leaves, fold each leaf in half, then with hand, pull stem toward top of leaf. Discard stems. Pack leaves into measuring cup to equal ¼ cup. Set aside.

3. To peel garlic, trim ends of garlic cloves. Slightly crush cloves, one at a time, under flat side of chef's knife blade; peel away skins.

4. Place basil leaves, garlic and peppers in jar.

continued on page 32

Italian Salad Dressing, continued

5. Place sherry in small saucepan. Bring just to a boil over medium-high heat. (Bubbles will begin to form on the surface of the sherry.) Remove saucepan from heat.

6. Pour sherry into jar; cover.

7. Shake jar several times to distribute basil leaves. Store in cool, dark place at least 7 days, shaking occasionally.

8. To transfer vinegar to clean, dry decorative glass bottle with tight-fitting lid, line a funnel with double layer of cheesecloth or coffee filter.

9. Place neck of funnel into bottle. Pour vinegar mixture into funnel. Save peppers and basil and add to bottle, if desired; cover. Store in cool, dark place up to 2 months.

Makes 2 cups

Barbecued Peanuts

2 tablespoons butter or margarine

¼ cup barbecue sauce

¾ teaspoon garlic salt

⅛ teaspoon cayenne pepper*

1 jar (16 ounces) dry roasted lightly salted peanuts

*For spicy Barbecued Peanuts, increase cayenne pepper to ¼ teaspoon.

1. Preheat oven to 325°F. Grease 13×9-inch baking pan. Set aside.

2. To melt butter, place butter in 1-cup glass measure. Microwave at MEDIUM (50% power) 1 minute or until butter is melted. Let stand 2 minutes.

3. Whisk melted butter, barbecue sauce, garlic salt and pepper in medium bowl with wire whisk until well blended. Add peanuts; toss until evenly coated with wooden spoon.

4. Spread peanuts in single layer in prepared baking pan.

5. Bake 20 to 22 minutes or until peanuts are glazed, stirring occasionally. Cool completely in pan on wire rack, stirring occasionally to prevent peanuts from sticking together.

6. Spoon into clean, dry decorative tin; cover.

7. Store tightly covered at room temperature up to 2 weeks.

Makes about 4 cups

Praline Pecans & Cranberries

3½ **cups pecan halves**
¼ **cup light corn syrup**
¼ **cup packed light brown sugar**
2 **tablespoons butter or margarine**
1 **teaspoon vanilla**
¼ **teaspoon baking soda**
1½ **cups dried cranberries or cherries**

1. Preheat oven to 250°F. Grease 13×9-inch baking pan. Cover large baking sheet with heavy-duty aluminum foil. Set aside.

2. Spread pecans in single layer in prepared baking pan.

3. Combine corn syrup, sugar and butter in 2-cup glass measure or small microwave-safe bowl. Microwave at HIGH 1 minute. Stir. Microwave 30 seconds to 1 minute or until boiling rapidly. Stir in vanilla and baking soda until well blended.

4. Drizzle evenly over pecans; stir with wooden spoon until evenly coated.

5. Bake 1 hour, stirring after each 20 minutes of baking with wooden spoon.

6. Immediately transfer mixture to prepared baking sheet, spreading pecans evenly over foil with lightly greased spatula.

7. Cool completely. Break pecans apart with wooden spoon. Combine pecans and cranberries in large bowl.

8. Store in airtight container at room temperature up to 2 weeks.

Makes about 5 cups

Caramel-Cinnamon Snack Mix

2 tablespoons vegetable oil
½ cup popcorn kernels
½ teaspoon salt, divided
1½ cups packed light brown sugar
½ cup butter or margarine
½ cup corn syrup
¼ cup red hot cinnamon candies
2 cups cinnamon-flavored bear-shaped graham crackers
1 cup red and green candy coated chocolate pieces

1. Grease 2 large baking pans. Set aside.

2. Heat oil in large saucepan over high heat until hot. Add corn kernels. Cover pan. Shake pan constantly over heat until kernels no longer pop.

3. Divide popcorn evenly between 2 large bowls. Add ¼ teaspoon salt to each bowl; toss to coat. Set aside.

4. Preheat oven to 250°F. Combine sugar, butter and corn syrup in heavy, medium saucepan. Cook over medium heat until sugar melts, stirring constantly with wooden spoon. Bring mixture to a boil. Boil 5 minutes, stirring frequently.

5. Remove ½ of sugar mixture (about ¾ cup) from saucepan; pour over 1 portion of popcorn. Toss with lightly greased spatula until evenly coated.

6. Add red hot candies to saucepan. Stir constantly with wooden spoon until melted. Pour over remaining portion of popcorn; toss with lightly greased spatula until evenly coated.

7. Spread each portion popcorn in even layer in separate prepared pans with lightly greased spatula.

8. Bake 1 hour, stirring every 15 minutes with wooden spoon to prevent popcorn from sticking together.

9. Cool completely in pans. Combine popcorn, graham crackers and chocolate pieces in large bowl.

10. Store in airtight container at room temperature up to 1 week.

Makes about 4 quarts

Nut Brittle

½ **cup peanut butter, toasted cashew butter or toasted almond butter**
1 **teaspoon baking soda**
1 **teaspoon vanilla**
1 **cup sugar**
1 **cup light corn syrup**
2 **tablespoons water**
1½ **cups raw peanuts, cashews or unblanched almonds**
½ **cup butter or margarine**

1. Bring 1 inch water in bottom of double boiler to a boil over high heat. Reduce heat to medium. Melt peanut butter in top of double boiler, stirring constantly with wooden spoon. Reduce heat to low. Let stand, stirring occasionally.

2. Lightly grease 16×14-inch baking sheet. Set aside. Blend baking soda and vanilla in small bowl until smooth.

3. Attach candy thermometer to side of medium saucepan, making sure bulb is not touching bottom of saucepan.

4. Combine sugar, corn syrup and water in saucepan. Bring to a boil over medium-high heat, stirring constantly. Add nuts and butter. Return to a boil, stirring constantly. Reduce heat to medium. Boil until temperature registers 280°F, stirring constantly.

5. Remove saucepan from heat. Stir in peanut butter with wooden spoon until well blended. Stir in vanilla mixture until well blended. Immediately pour mixture evenly over prepared baking sheet.

6. Quickly roll out brittle with buttered rolling pin to as thin as possible. Cool completely on baking sheet.

7. Break into pieces. Store tightly covered at room temperature up to 1 week.   *Makes about 1½ pounds*

Apple-Cheddar Scones

1 apple
1 recipe Apple-Cheddar Scone Mix (recipe follows)
6 tablespoons cold butter, cut into pieces
½ cup plus 2 tablespoons shredded Cheddar cheese, divided

1. Preheat oven to 400°F. Lightly grease large baking sheet. Set aside.

2. To peel apple, hold apple in one hand and peel off skin in strips with sharp knife or peeler.

3. To remove core, insert apple corer into center of apple. Push completely through bottom of apple; pull apple corer from apple to remove. Discard core and seeds.

4. To chop apple, cut into quarters; cut quarters into small pieces with utility knife.

5. Pour scone mix into large bowl. Cut in butter with pastry blender until mixture resembles coarse crumbs. Stir in apple and ½ cup cheese with wooden spoon. Stir in ½ cup water until soft dough forms; form into ball.

6. Place dough on prepared baking sheet. Press into 8-inch round with lightly floured hands. Cut into 8 wedges with lightly floured knife; slightly separate pieces by moving knife back and forth between slices. Sprinkle remaining 2 tablespoons cheese evenly over wedges.

7. Bake 20 minutes or until lightly browned. Remove scones with spatula to wire rack; cool completely. Store in airtight container at room temperature up to 3 days.

Makes 8 scones

Apple-Cheddar Scone Mix

1¾ cups all-purpose flour
2 tablespoons powdered buttermilk
1 tablespoon sugar
1 teaspoon baking powder
¼ teaspoon baking soda
¼ teaspoon salt
¾ teaspoon dried thyme leaves

Combine all ingredients in small bowl until well blended. Store in airtight container at room temperature up to 3 months.

Makes about 2 cups

Pumpkin-Pecan Friendship Bread

3 cups chopped pecans, divided
1 can (16 ounces) solid-pack pumpkin
1 cup Starter (recipe follows)
4 eggs
½ cup vegetable oil
2 teaspoons vanilla
3 cups all-purpose flour
1 cup granulated sugar
1 cup packed light brown sugar
4 teaspoons ground cinnamon
2 teaspoons baking powder
1 teaspoon baking soda
1 teaspoon ground nutmeg
1 teaspoon ground ginger
1 teaspoon ground cloves

1. Preheat oven to 350°F. Grease and flour 2 (9½×4-inch) loaf pans. Set aside.

2. Reserve 1 cup pecans. Spread remaining 2 cups pecans in single layer in large baking pan. Bake 8 minutes or until golden brown, stirring frequently.

3. Combine pumpkin, Starter, eggs, oil and vanilla in large bowl. Combine remaining ingredients in separate large bowl until well blended. Stir into pumpkin mixture just until blended. Stir in toasted pecans. Spoon batter evenly into prepared pans. Sprinkle reserved pecans evenly over batter.

4. Bake 1 hour or until wooden pick inserted in centers comes out clean. Cool in pans on wire rack 5 minutes. Remove from pans. Cool completely on wire rack. Wrap in plastic wrap. Store at room temperature up to 1 week.

Makes 2 loaves

Starter

1 cup sugar
1 cup all-purpose flour
1 cup milk

1. Combine all ingredients in large resealable plastic food storage bag. Knead bag until well blended. Let bag stand *at room temperature* 5 days. Knead bag 5 times each day.

2. On day 6, add 1 cup sugar, 1 cup flour and 1 cup milk. Knead bag until well blended. Let stand *at room temperature* 4 days. Knead bag 5 times each day.

3. On day 10, pour 1 cup Starter into each of 3 bags. Reserve remaining 1 cup Starter for recipe. Give remaining bags of Starter with recipe as gifts.

Makes about 4 cups

Cherry, Almond & Chocolate Breakfast Wreath

1 cup dry sweet or
    sour cherries
½ cup sugar, divided
¼ cup warm water
    (105° to 115°F)
1 package active
    dry yeast
½ cup plus 1
    tablespoon
    milk, divided
3 tablespoons
    butter or
    margarine, cut
    into pieces
2 eggs, divided
1 tablespoon grated
    lemon peel
    (page 49)
½ teaspoon salt
½ teaspoon almond
    extract
2½ to 2¾ cups all-
    purpose flour
½ cup canned
    almond filling
    (about
    12 ounces)
¾ cup semisweet
    chocolate chips
    Almond Glaze
    (page 48)

1. Grease large bowl and large baking sheet. Set aside. Combine 1 cup water, cherries and ¼ cup sugar in small saucepan. Bring to a boil over high heat, stirring constantly with wooden spoon. Cover saucepan; remove from heat. Set aside.

2. Pour ¼ cup warm water into large bowl. Sprinkle yeast over water. Let stand 5 minutes. Stir with wooden spoon to dissolve.

3. Meanwhile heat ½ cup milk and butter in medium saucepan over high heat until milk bubbles around edge of saucepan, stirring constantly with wooden spoon (butter does not need to melt completely). Remove saucepan from heat; stir occasionally until milk is warm to touch.

4. Add milk mixture to yeast mixture. Stir in remaining ¼ cup sugar, 1 egg, lemon peel, salt and almond extract until well blended. Add 2¼ cups flour; stir until dough forms sticky ball. Stir in enough remaining flour until soft dough forms.

5. Place dough on lightly floured surface. Knead dough with lightly floured hands 5 minutes or until smooth and elastic, adding additional flour to prevent sticking if necessary. Shape dough into ball; place in prepared bowl, turning dough to completely cover in grease. Cover bowl with plastic wrap; let rise in warm place 1 to 2 hours or until dough doubles in bulk.

6. Preheat oven to 350°F. Punch down dough several times. Turn out dough onto lightly floured surface. Knead dough with lightly floured hands 10 to 12 times or until dough is smooth. Shape dough into 10-inch-long log. Flatten slightly.

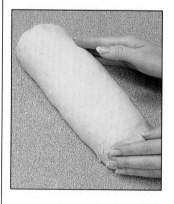

continued on page 48

Cherry, Almond & Chocolate Breakfast Wreath, *continued*

7. Roll out dough into 18×8-inch rectangle with lightly floured rolling pin. Trim ½-inch-thick strip of dough from short (8-inch) ends of rectangle with sharp knife; set aside strips for decorating wreath.

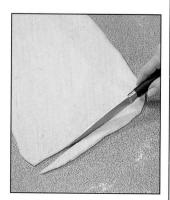

8. Starting ½ inch from long (18-inch) edge that is furthest from you, spread almond filling evenly over dough with spatula. Sprinkle cherries and chocolate evenly over filling. Beginning at long edge nearest you, roll up dough jelly-roll style. Pinch seam along length to seal.

9. Carefully place roll on prepared baking sheet, curving into 8-inch diameter circle. Pinch ends together.

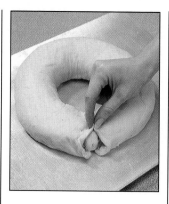

10. Cut dough at 1½-inch intervals to within ¾ inch of center with sharp knife. Gently lift each section and turn on its side, overlapping slices.

11. Beat remaining egg and remaining 1 tablespoon milk in small bowl with fork until well blended. Brush lightly over wreath.

12. To decorate wreath, cut 1 reserved dough strip into 15 or 18 pieces. Roll pieces into balls; place on wreath in clusters of three. Roll remaining dough strip into 12-inch-long log; shape into bow. Place bow on wreath. Brush berries and bow with egg mixture.

13. Bake 30 minutes or until wreath is golden brown. (If outer edge browns more rapidly than inner edge of circle, cover outer edge with heavy-duty foil. Bake until inner edge is golden brown.) Cool on baking sheet 5 minutes. Remove from pan to wire rack. Cool completely. Prepare Almond Glaze; drizzle over wreath with spoon. Let stand until set. Wrap in plastic wrap. Store at room temperature up to 1 week.

Makes 1 wreath

Almond Glaze

½ **cup powdered sugar, sifted**
2 **teaspoons milk**
¼ **teaspoon almond extract**

Combine all ingredients in small bowl; add additional milk until just thickened.

Makes about ¼ cup

Sour Cream Coffee Cake

Streusel Topping (page 50)
1 lemon
¾ cup sugar
6 tablespoons butter or margarine
2 eggs
1 cup sour cream
1½ teaspoons vanilla
1½ cups all-purpose flour
1½ teaspoons ground cardamom
1 teaspoon baking powder
1 teaspoon baking soda
⅛ teaspoon salt
Cranberry Sauce (page 50)

1. Prepare Streusel Topping. Set aside. Grease and flour bottom and side of 8-inch springform pan.

2. Finely grate colored portion of lemon peel using bell grater or hand-held grater. Measure 1 tablespoon lemon peel.

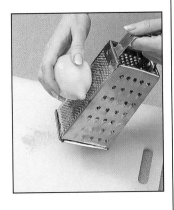

3. Preheat oven to 350°F. Beat sugar and butter in large bowl with electric mixer at medium speed until light and fluffy, scraping down side of bowl once. Beat in eggs, 1 at a time, until well blended. Beat in sour cream, vanilla and lemon peel. Add flour, cardamom, baking powder, baking soda and salt; beat at low speed just until blended, scraping down side of bowl occasionally.

4. Spoon half of batter into prepared pan. Sprinkle half of streusel over batter. Repeat layers ending with streusel.

5. Bake 50 to 60 minutes or until wooden pick inserted in center comes out clean. Cool in pan on wire rack 15 minutes.

6. Run long slender knife around edge of pan to loosen cake. Unhinge side; lift off. Cool until cake is just warm to touch.

7. Slide long slender knife under cake; rotate cake to loosen from bottom. Slide off onto serving plate. Serve slices of coffee cake with Cranberry Sauce.

8. Wrap in plastic wrap. Store at room temperature up to 1 week.

Makes 10 servings

continued on page 50

Sour Cream Coffee Cake, continued

Streusel Topping

¾ cup chopped walnuts or pecans

⅓ cup packed light brown sugar

2 tablespoons all-purpose flour

½ teaspoon ground cardamom

½ teaspoon ground nutmeg

½ teaspoon ground cinnamon

3 tablespoons butter or margarine, melted

Combine walnuts, sugar, flour, cardamom, nutmeg and cinnamon in small bowl. Stir in butter until well blended.

Makes about ¾ cup

Cranberry Sauce

2 cups fresh or thawed frozen cranberries, drained

1 cup orange juice

¾ cup sugar

2 teaspoons cornstarch

2 teaspoons water

1 tablespoon grated lemon peel (page 49)

2 to 3 tablespoons cranberry- or orange-flavored liqueur (optional)

1. Combine cranberries, orange juice and sugar in medium saucepan. Bring to a boil over high heat, stirring frequently with wooden spoon. Reduce heat to medium-low. Cover; simmer 10 minutes or until cranberries are tender and pop. Remove saucepan from heat.

2. Remove ½ of cranberries from saucepan; reserve in medium bowl. Mash remaining cranberries with back of spoon.

3. Blend cornstarch and water in small bowl until smooth. Add cornstarch mixture and lemon peel to saucepan; blend well.

4. Simmer mixture over medium heat 2 minutes or until thickened, stirring frequently. Stir in reserved whole cranberries. Remove saucepan from heat. Cool completely. Stir in liqueur to taste.

5. Store in airtight container in refrigerator up to 3 weeks.

Makes about 2 cups

Chunky Applesauce

10 tart apples (about 3 pounds)
¾ cup packed light brown sugar
½ cup apple juice or apple cider
1½ teaspoons ground cinnamon
⅛ teaspoon salt
⅛ teaspoon ground nutmeg

1. To peel apple, hold apple in hand and peel off skin in strips with sharp knife or peeler. Repeat with remaining apples.

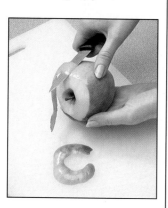

2. To remove core, center apple corer over top of apple. Push completely through bottom of apple. Discard core and seeds. Repeat with remaining apples.

3. To chop apple, cut into quarters with utility knife; cut quarters into small pieces. Repeat with remaining apples.

4. Combine apples, brown sugar, apple juice, cinnamon, salt and nutmeg in heavy, large saucepan; cover. Cook over medium-low heat 40 to 45 minutes or until apples are tender, stirring occasionally with wooden spoon to break apples into chunks. Remove saucepan from heat. Cool completely.

5. Store in airtight container in refrigerator up to 1 month.

Makes about 5½ cups

Turtle Caramel Apples

4 large Golden
    Delicious
    apples
2 jars (3½ ounces
    each)
    macadamia nuts
    or pecans
1 package
    (14 ounces)
    caramels,
    unwrapped
1 bittersweet or
    semisweet
    chocolate candy
    bar (about 2
    ounces), broken
    into small
    pieces
EQUIPMENT:
    Craft sticks

1. Line 13×9-inch baking pan with waxed paper; set aside.

2. To prepare apples, wash and dry completely. Remove stems. Insert craft sticks into centers of apples.

3. To coarsely chop nuts, place nuts in work bowl of food processor. Process using on/off pulsing action until nuts are coarsely chopped. Place nuts in medium bowl. Set aside.

4. To melt caramels, combine caramels and 2 tablespoons water in small saucepan. Simmer over low heat until caramels melt and mixture is smooth, stirring frequently with wooden spoon.

5. Immediately dip apples, one at a time, into caramel to cover completely. Scrape excess caramel from bottom of apple onto side of saucepan, letting excess drip back into saucepan.

continued on page 56

Turtle Caramel Apples, *continued*

6. Immediately roll apples in nuts to lightly coat, pressing nuts lightly with fingers so they stick to caramel.

7. Place apples, stick-side up, on prepared baking sheet. Let stand 20 minutes or until caramel is set.

8. To melt chocolate, place chocolate in small resealable plastic freezer bag; seal bag. Microwave at MEDIUM (50% power) 1 minute. Turn bag over; microwave at MEDIUM 1 minute or until melted. Knead bag until chocolate is smooth.

9. Cut off very tiny corner of bag; pipe or drizzle chocolate decoratively onto apples.

10. Let apples stand 30 minutes or until chocolate is set.

11. Store loosely covered in refrigerator up to 3 days. Let stand at room temperature 15 minutes before serving.

Makes 4 apples

Best Ever Apple Pie

2⅓ cups all-purpose
     flour, divided
  ¾ cup plus 1
     tablespoon
     sugar, divided
  ½ teaspoon baking
     powder
  ½ teaspoon salt
  ¾ cup cold unsalted
     butter
  4 to 5 tablespoons
     ice water
  1 egg white (page 8)
  7 medium apples
     such as
     Jonathan,
     Macintosh or
     Granny Smith,
     peeled, cored,
     sliced (page 42)
  1 tablespoon lemon
     juice
1¼ teaspoons ground
     cinnamon
  3 tablespoons
     unsalted butter,
     cut into small
     pieces
  1 egg yolk (page 8)
  1 tablespoon sour
     cream

1. Combine 2 cups flour, 1 tablespoon sugar, baking powder and salt in large bowl until well blended. Cut in butter using pastry blender or 2 knives until mixture resembles coarse crumbs.

2. Add water, 1 tablespoon at a time, to flour mixture. Toss with fork until mixture holds together. Form dough into 2 (6-inch) discs. Wrap discs in plastic wrap; refrigerate 30 minutes or until firm.

3. Working with 1 disc at a time, unwrap dough and place on lightly floured surface. Roll out dough in short strokes, starting in the middle of disc and rolling out towards edge with lightly floured rolling pin.

4. Rotate dough ¼ turn to the right. Sprinkle more flour under dough and on rolling pin as necessary to prevent sticking.

5. Roll out dough into 12-inch circle, ⅛ inch thick.

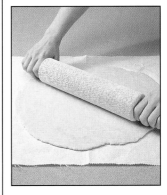

6. Place rolling pin on one side of dough. Gently roll dough over rolling pin once.

continued on page 58

Best Ever Apple Pie, continued

7. Carefully lift rolling pin and dough, unrolling dough over 9-inch glass pie plate.

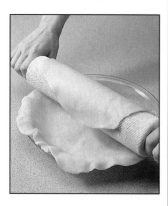

8. Ease dough into pie plate with fingertips. *Do not stretch dough.* Trim dough leaving ½-inch overhang; brush with egg white. Set aside.

9. Preheat oven to 450°F. Place apple slices in large bowl; sprinkle with lemon juice. Combine remaining ⅓ cup flour, ¾ cup sugar and cinnamon in small bowl with wooden spoon until well blended. Add to apple mixture; toss to coat apples evenly. Spoon filling into prepared pie crust; place butter on top of filling.

10. Moisten edge of dough with water. Roll out remaining disc as described in Steps 3 to 5. Place onto filled pie as described in Steps 6 and 7. Trim dough leaving ½-inch overhang.

11. To flute, press dough between thumb and forefinger to make stand-up edge. Cut slits in dough at ½-inch intervals around edge to form flaps.

12. Press 1 flap in toward center of pie and the next out toward rim of pie plate. Continue alternating in and out around edge of pie.

13. Cut 4 small slits in top of dough with paring knife to allow steam to escape.

14. Combine egg yolk and sour cream in small bowl until well blended. Cover; refrigerate until ready to use.

15. Bake 10 minutes; *reduce oven temperature to 375°F.* Bake 35 minutes. Brush egg yolk mixture evenly on pie crust with pastry brush. Bake 20 to 25 minutes or until crust is deep golden brown.

16. Cool pie completely in pie plate on wire rack.

17. Store loosely covered at room temperature 1 day or refrigerate up to 4 days.

Makes 1 (9-inch) pie

Gingered Apple-Cranberry Chutney

2 medium Granny
    Smith apples
1 package
    (12 ounces)
    fresh or thawed
    frozen
    cranberries
1¼ cups packed light
    brown sugar
¾ cup cranberry
    juice cocktail
½ cup golden raisins
¼ cup chopped
    crystallized
    ginger
¼ cup cider vinegar
1 teaspoon ground
    cinnamon
⅛ teaspoon ground
    allspice

1. To peel apple, hold apple in hand and peel off skin in strips with sharp knife or peeler. Repeat with remaining apple.

2. To remove core, insert apple corer into center of apple. Push completely through bottom of apple; pull apple corer from apple to remove. Discard core and seeds. Repeat with remaining apple.

3. To chop apple, cut into quarters; cut quarters into small pieces with utility knife. Repeat with remaining apple.

4. Combine apples, cranberries, sugar, cranberry juice cocktail, raisins, ginger, vinegar, cinnamon and allspice in heavy, medium saucepan. Bring to a boil over high heat. Reduce heat to medium. Simmer 20 to 25 minutes or until mixture is very thick, stirring occasionally with wooden spoon.

5. Remove saucepan from heat. Cool completely.

6. Store in airtight container in refrigerator up to 2 weeks.

Makes about 3 cups

Triple Layer Fudge

Chocolate Fudge (recipe follows)
Peanut Butter Fudge (recipe follows)
White Fudge (recipe follows)

1. Grease 13×9-inch baking pan. Set aside. Prepare Chocolate Fudge. Immediately spread into prepared pan with lightly greased rubber spatula.

2. Immediately prepare Peanut Butter Fudge; spread evenly over Chocolate Fudge with lightly greased rubber spatula.

3. Immediately prepare White Fudge; spread evenly over Peanut Butter Fudge with lightly greased spatula.

4. If desired, to marble fudge, swirl knife through all layers, lifting and turning fudge with each swirl.

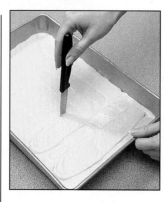

5. Cover fudge with plastic wrap. Refrigerate 2 hours or until firm. Cut into 1-inch squares. Store tightly covered in refrigerator up to 3 weeks.

Makes about 10 dozen pieces

Chocolate Fudge

1½ cups granulated sugar
1 can (5 ounces) evaporated milk
2 tablespoons butter or margarine
¼ teaspoon salt
1½ cups miniature marshmallows
1 cup (6 ounces) semisweet chocolate chips
1½ teaspoons vanilla

1. Combine sugar, milk, butter and salt in medium saucepan. Bring to a boil over medium heat, stirring constantly with wooden spoon. Boil 5 minutes, stirring constantly.

2. Remove saucepan from heat. Stir in marshmallows with wooden spoon until melted and mixture is well blended.

3. Add chocolate chips and vanilla. Stir until mixture is smooth. Stir mixture 6 minutes or until slightly thickened.

Peanut Butter Fudge

Reduce granulated sugar to ¾ cup; *add* ¾ cup packed light brown sugar. *Omit* butter and chocolate. Prepare as directed for Chocolate Fudge in Steps 1 and 2. Stir ½ cup creamy peanut butter into mixture as directed in Step 3.

White Fudge

Substitute white chocolate chips for semisweet chocolate chips. Prepare as directed for Chocolate Fudge.

Chocolate-Dipped Delights

1 cup chopped toasted almonds (page 88)
1⅔ cups (about 10 ounces) chopped white chocolate
2 cups (about 12 ounces) chopped semisweet chocolate
1⅔ cups (about 10 ounces) chopped milk chocolate
3 tablespoons shortening, divided
Heart-shaped pretzels
Biscotti
Chocolate sandwich cookies
Decorator Frosting (page 16)
Liquid food coloring
Ridged potato chips
EQUIPMENT:
Small paint brushes

1. Place nuts in medium bowl. Set aside. To melt chocolate, place each chocolate and 1 tablespoon shortening in separate 4-cup glass measures. Microwave, 1 measure at a time, at MEDIUM (50% power) 4 to 5 minutes or until chocolate is melted, stirring after 2 minutes.

2. Place large sheet waxed paper on counter. Dip ½ of each pretzel into white chocolate. Gently shake off excess chocolate; place on waxed paper. Let stand 10 minutes; repeat. Let stand 30 minutes or until set.

3. Dip other halves of pretzels into semisweet chocolate. Place on waxed paper. Let stand until set.

4. Spread milk chocolate on curved edge of biscotti with small knife. Roll in nuts. Place on waxed paper. Let stand 30 minutes or until set.

5. Holding cookie flat, dip 1 side of each cookie into semisweet chocolate. Shake off excess chocolate. Place on waxed paper. Let stand 30 minutes or until set. Repeat with second side.

6. Prepare Decorator Frosting. Tint with liquid food coloring, if desired. Pipe design on cookies, if desired.

7. To paint potato chips, dip paint brush into milk chocolate. Paint chocolate onto 1 side of each chip. Let stand 30 minutes or until set.

8. Store loosely covered at room temperature up to 1 week.

Makes 3 cups melted chocolate

Killer Brownies

½ cup hazelnuts or unblanched almonds

¾ cup butter or margarine

2 cups sugar

¾ cup cocoa powder

3 eggs, slightly beaten

2 teaspoons vanilla

1 cup all-purpose flour

1½ cups fresh or thawed frozen raspberries

White Chocolate Ganache (page 68)

Chocolate Ganache (page 68)

3 to 4 tablespoons raspberry jam

1. Preheat oven to 350°F. To remove skins from nuts, spread in single layer on baking sheet. Bake 10 to 12 minutes or until skins begin to flake off; let cool slightly. Wrap hazelnuts in heavy kitchen towel; rub against towel to remove as much of the skins as possible.

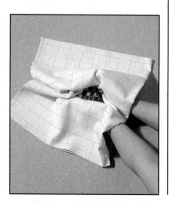

2. Place hazelnuts in work bowl of food processor. Process using on/off pulsing action until hazelnuts are finely chopped, but not pasty. Set aside.

3. Lightly grease 2 (8-inch) square baking pans. Line bottoms of pans with foil; lightly grease foil. Set aside.

4. Melt butter in medium saucepan over medium heat, stirring occasionally with wooden spoon. Remove saucepan from heat. Stir in sugar and cocoa powder until well blended. Stir in eggs and vanilla until smooth. Stir in flour just until blended. Pour batter evenly into prepared pans. Place raspberries on top of batter, pressing gently into batter.

5. Bake 15 to 20 minutes or until center is just set. *Do not overbake.* Cool brownies completely in pans on wire rack.

6. Run knife around edges of pans to loosen brownies from sides. Gently work flexible metal spatula down edges and slightly under brownies to loosen from bottoms of pans. Hold wire rack over top of 1 pan; invert to release brownie. Remove foil; discard. Lay cutting board or plate over brownie; invert brownie.

continued on page 68

Killer Brownies, continued

7. Prepare White Chocolate Ganache and Chocolate Ganache. Reserve 2 tablespoons White Chocolate Ganache; spread remaining White Chocolate Ganache evenly on brownie with spatula. Spread raspberry jam on top of ganache.

8. Unmold remaining brownie as directed in Step 6. Place flat-side down on bottom layer, pressing gently to seal. Spread Chocolate Ganache evenly on top layer with spatula. Drizzle reserved 2 tablespoons White Chocolate Ganache over Chocolate Ganache with spoon. Sprinkle with hazelnuts. Cut into 16 squares.

9. Store tightly covered in refrigerator up to 1 week.

Makes 16 brownies

White Chocolate Ganache

　1 cup (6 ounces) white chocolate chips or chopped white chocolate, divided
　3 tablespoons whipping cream
　½ teaspoon almond extract

1. Combine ½ cup chocolate and whipping cream in medium saucepan. Heat over medium heat until chocolate is half melted, stirring occasionally with wooden spoon.

2. Remove saucepan from heat. Stir in remaining ½ cup chocolate and almond extract until mixture is smooth. Keep warm (ganache is semi-firm at room temperature).

Makes ¾ cup

Chocolate Ganache

　2 tablespoons whipping cream
　1 tablespoon butter
　½ cup (2 ounces) semisweet chocolate chips or chopped semisweet chocolate
　½ teaspoon vanilla

Combine whipping cream and butter in small saucepan. Heat over medium heat until mixture boils, stirring frequently with wooden spoon. Remove saucepan from heat. Stir in chocolate and vanilla until mixture is smooth, returning to heat for 20 to 30 second intervals as needed to melt chocolate. Keep warm (ganache is semi-firm at room temperature).

Makes about ½ cup

Truffles

Dark Chocolate Truffles

1⅔ **cups chopped semisweet chocolate or semisweet chocolate chips**

6 **tablespoons whipping cream***

1 **tablespoon cold butter or margarine, cut into pieces**

1 **teaspoon vanilla**

½ **cup chopped macadamia nuts or toffee, or chocolate decors**

*To flavor with liqueur, reduce cream to ¼ cup. Stir 2 tablespoons liqueur into chocolate mixture along with vanilla.

1. Place chocolate in small bowl. Combine whipping cream and butter in small saucepan. Simmer over medium-high heat until butter melts, stirring constantly with wooden spoon. Pour over chocolate; stir once.

2. Cover bowl; let stand 3 to 5 minutes. Uncover; stir until chocolate is melted and mixture is smooth. Stir in vanilla and liqueur, if using. Cover. Refrigerate 15 minutes or until mixture is firm enough to hold its shape.

3. Place 18 level tablespoonfuls mixture on plate. Cover; refrigerate 2 hours or until fudgy, but not soft.

4. Place nuts in medium bowl. To make Truffles, roll each tablespoon chocolate mixture into ball. Roll Truffles in coating to evenly coat. (Warm hands and room temperature quickly soften chocolate, making it difficult to form balls. Keeping chocolate chilled prevents sticking.)

5. Store tightly covered in refrigerator up to 3 weeks. Serve chilled or let stand at room temperature 15 to 20 minutes before serving.

Makes 18 truffles

continued on page 70

Truffles, continued

White Chocolate Truffles

1⅔ cups (10 ounces) chopped white chocolate or white chocolate chips
¼ cup whipping cream*
½ teaspoon vanilla
½ cup chopped macadamia nuts or toffee, or chocolate decors

*To flavor with liqueur, reduce cream to 2 tablespoons. Stir 2 tablespoons hazelnut- or almond-flavored liqueur into chocolate mixture along with vanilla.

1. Place chocolate in small bowl. Place whipping cream in small saucepan. Simmer over medium-high heat until heated through, stirring constantly with wooden spoon. Pour over chocolate, stir once.

2. Cover bowl; let stand 3 to 5 minutes. Uncover; stir until chocolate is melted and mixture is smooth. Stir in vanilla and liqueur, if using. Cover. Refrigerate 15 minutes or until mixture is firm enough to hold its shape.

3. Shape and coat truffles as directed in Steps 3 to 5 on page 69.

Makes 18 truffles

Gianduia Truffles

6 tablespoons butter or margarine*
6 ounces (1 cup) chopped milk chocolate or milk chocolate chips
1 cup toasted hazelnuts or unblanched almonds (page 66)
½ cup chopped macadamia nuts or toffee, or chocolate decors

*To flavor with liqueur, reduce butter to 2 tablespoons. Stir 2 tablespoons hazelnut- or almond-flavored liqueur into melted chocolate mixture.

1. Melt butter in small saucepan over low heat, stirring occasionally with wooden spoon.

2. Remove saucepan from heat. Add chocolate; stir until melted. Stir in nuts. Refrigerate 15 minutes or until firm.

3. Shape and coat truffles as directed in Steps 3 to 5 on page 69.

Makes 18 truffles

Almond-Cranberry Syrup

1 package
　(12 ounces)
　frozen
　cranberries,
　thawed
1 cup sugar
¾ cup corn syrup
¼ teaspoon almond
　extract
　(optional)

1. Combine cranberries and ¼ cup water in medium saucepan. Bring to a boil over high heat. Boil 10 minutes or until cranberries are tender and pop, stirring frequently with wooden spoon.

2. Add sugar and corn syrup to saucepan. Bring to a boil over high heat. Boil 10 minutes or until mixture thickens and coats wooden spoon, stirring constantly. Remove saucepan from heat.

3. Place wire mesh sieve over medium bowl. Pour cranberry mixture into sieve, pressing cranberries with back of wooden spoon to extract all of juices. Cool completely. Reserve cranberries for another use.*

4. When syrup has cooled completely, strain again in wire mesh sieve; discard solids.

5. To transfer syrup to clean, dry decorative glass bottle, place neck of funnel in bottle. Pour syrup into funnel. Remove funnel; seal bottle.

6. Store in airtight container in refrigerator up to 2 months.

Makes about 1¾ cups

*Spoon cranberries into clean, dry decorative jar; cover. Serve as a spread.

Buckwheat Pancakes

Almond-Cranberry Syrup

Citrus Butter

1 cup butter
1 orange
1 lime

1. To soften butter, place butter on opened packages on cutting board. Cut butter lengthwise into ½-inch slices with utility knife. Cut crosswise into ½-inch pieces. Let stand at room temperature until softened.

2. Meanwhile, finely grate colored portion of orange peel using bell grater or hand-held grater. Measure ¾ teaspoon orange peel. Set aside.

3. To juice orange, cut orange in half on cutting board with utility knife. Remove any visible seeds with tip of knife. Using citrus reamer, squeeze juice from orange halves into measuring cup or small bowl. Measure 2 tablespoons. Set aside.

4. Finely grate colored portion of lime peel using bell grater or hand-held grater. Measure ¼ teaspoon lime peel.

5. Combine butter, orange peel, orange juice and lime peel in medium bowl with electric mixer. Beat at medium speed until well blended.

6. Spoon butter mixture into clean, dry decorative crock, packing down with back of wooden spoon; cover.

7. Or, place butter mixture on sheet of waxed paper. Using waxed paper to hold butter mixture, roll it back and forth to form a log. Wrap log in plastic wrap.

8. Store in airtight container in refrigerator up to 2 weeks.

Makes about 1 cup

Serving Note: Remove desired amount from crock or roll; immediately refrigerate remaining butter.

Honey Butter
Omit orange peel, orange juice and lime peel. Substitute ¼ cup honey.

Strawberry Butter
Omit orange peel, orange juice and lime peel. Substitute ⅔ cup strawberry preserves.

Fruited Granola

3 cups uncooked quick-cooking oats
1 cup sliced unblanched almonds
3 tablespoons butter or margarine
1 cup honey
½ cup wheat germ or honey wheat germ
1 teaspoon ground cinnamon
3 cups whole grain or whole wheat cereal flakes
½ cup dried blueberries or golden raisins
½ cup dried cranberries or tart cherries
½ cup dried banana chips or chopped pitted dates

1. Preheat oven to 325°F. Spread oats and almonds in single layer in 13×9-inch baking pan. Bake 15 minutes or until lightly toasted, stirring frequently with wooden spoon. Remove pan from oven. Set aside.

2. To melt butter, place butter in 1-cup glass measure. Microwave at MEDIUM (50% power) 1 minute or until butter is melted. Let stand 2 minutes.

3. Combine honey, melted butter, wheat germ and cinnamon in large bowl with wooden spoon until well blended. Add oats and almonds; toss to coat completely. Spread mixture in single layer in baking pan with wooden spoon.

4. Bake 20 minutes or until golden brown. Cool completely in pan on wire rack. Break mixture into chunks with wooden spoon.

5. Combine oat chunks, cereal, blueberries, cranberries and banana chips in large bowl.

6. Store in airtight container at room temperature up to 2 weeks.

Makes about 10 cups

Spiced Peach Sauce

2 pounds frozen
    sliced
    unsweetened
    peaches
1 lemon
2 cups sugar
1½ teaspoons ground
    cinnamon
¼ teaspoon ground
    nutmeg

1. To quickly thaw peaches, place frozen peaches in large resealable plastic food storage bag; seal bag. Place bag in large bowl of cold water until completely thawed.

2. To juice lemon, cut lemon in half with utility knife on cutting board; with tip of knife, remove any visible seeds. Repeat with remaining lemon half.

3. Using citrus reamer or squeezing tightly with hand, squeeze juice from lemon half into small bowl. Remove any remaining seeds from bowl. Repeat with remaining lemon half. Measure 1½ tablespoons.

4. Combine peaches and thawing liquid, sugar, lemon juice, cinnamon and nutmeg in heavy, medium saucepan.

5. Bring to a boil over high heat. Boil 45 to 50 minutes or until thickened, stirring occasionally and breaking peaches into small pieces with back of wooden spoon. Remove saucepan from heat; cool completely.

6. Store in airtight container in refrigerator up to 2 months.

Makes about 3 cups

Buckwheat Pancakes

1 cup Buckwheat Pancake Mix (recipe follows)
2 tablespoons butter
1 cup milk
1 egg, slightly beaten

1. Place pancake mix in medium bowl; make well in center.

2. To melt butter, place in glass measure. Microwave at MEDIUM (50% power) 1 minute or until melted. Let stand 2 minutes.

3. Blend milk, melted butter and egg in small bowl with wire whisk. Pour into well.

4. Stir with wooden spoon just until blended. (Batter will have small lumps.)

5. Lightly grease griddle or skillet with butter or nonstick cooking spray.

6. Heat griddle until hot. To test the heat of griddle or skillet, sprinkle a few drops of water onto surface of griddle. When the drops sizzle, the griddle is ready to use.

7. To make pancakes, drop ¼-cupfuls of batter onto hot griddle. Cook 3 to 4 minutes or until bubbles appear and break on the surface of pancakes.

8. Turn pancakes with metal spatula. Cook 3 to 4 minutes or until bottoms are browned. (To check for doneness, gently lift bottom of pancake with metal spatula.) Serve immediately.

Makes about 12 pancakes

Buttermilk Pancakes
Substitute 1¼ cups buttermilk for milk.

Blueberry Pancakes
Fold ½ cup fresh or thawed frozen blueberries into batter.

Buckwheat Pancake Mix
  2 cups buckwheat flour*
  2 cups all-purpose flour
  2 tablespoons sugar
  4 teaspoons baking powder
  2 teaspoons baking soda
  1 teaspoon salt

*Buckwheat flour can be purchased in health food stores. Substitute whole wheat flour, if desired.

Combine all ingredients in medium bowl until well blended. Store in airtight container at room temperature up to 2 months.

Makes about 4 cups

Prefab Gingerbread House

Gingerbread House Cookies

- 1 cup butter or shortening
- 1 cup packed brown sugar
- 1 cup dark molasses
- 1 egg
- 1 tablespoon ground ginger
- 1 teaspoon salt
- 1 teaspoon baking soda
- 1 teaspoon ground cinnamon
- 1 teaspoon ground allspice
- ½ teaspoon ground cloves
- 5 to 5½ cups all-purpose flour

EQUIPMENT AND DECORATIONS:

- Pencil
- Tracing paper
- Scissors
- Cardboard
- Bubble wrap
- Meringue powder* (optional)
- Assorted candies and decors (optional)
- Packing peanuts

*Meringue powder is available where cake decorating supplies are sold.

1. Draw patterns for house pieces using diagrams on page 85 as guides. To make larger or smaller house, enlarge or reduce patterns on copy machine. Trace patterns onto cardboard paper; cut out 2 pieces from each pattern.

2. Beat butter and sugar in large bowl with electric mixer at medium speed until light and fluffy. Beat in molasses until well blended. Beat in egg until well blended, scraping down side of bowl occasionally. Beat in ginger, salt, baking soda, cinnamon, allspice and cloves until well blended. Beat in 2 cups flour at low speed until well blended, scraping down side of bowl once. Gradually beat in remaining 3 to 3½ cups flour until stiff dough forms.

3. Form dough into 2 discs. Square corners. Wrap discs in plastic wrap. Refrigerate 1 hour or until dough is firm.

4. Preheat oven to 375°F. Lightly grease 1 or 2 (16×14-inch) baking sheets. Working with 1 disc at a time, unwrap dough and place in center of baking sheet. Roll out dough evenly to cover entire baking sheet with lightly greased rolling pin.

5. Place sheet of waxed paper over dough to prevent dough from sticking to pattern pieces. Lay pattern pieces on waxed paper at least 1 inch apart. Cut dough around patterns with sharp knife; remove patterns and waxed paper. Lift scraps from sheet; press together. Wrap in plastic wrap. Refrigerate until ready to use.

continued on page 84

Canned Peanut Butter Candy Cookies

¾ **cup chunky peanut butter**
½ **cup butter or margarine, softened (page 74)**
1 **cup packed light brown sugar**
½ **teaspoon baking powder**
½ **teaspoon baking soda**
1 **egg**
1½ **teaspoons vanilla**
1¼ **cups all-purpose flour**
2 **cups quartered miniature peanut butter cups**
⅓ **cup milk chocolate chips or chopped milk chocolate bar**

EQUIPMENT:
Decorative container

1. Beat peanut butter and butter in large bowl with electric mixer at medium speed until well blended. Beat in sugar, baking powder and baking soda until well blended. Beat in egg and vanilla until well blended. Beat in flour at low speed just until combined, scraping down side of bowl once. Stir in peanut butter cups with wooden spoon. Cover with plastic wrap. Refrigerate 1 hour or until firm.

2. Preheat oven to 375°F. For test cookie, measure inside diameter of container. Form ⅓ cup dough into ¼-inch-thick disc, about 2 inches in diameter less than the diameter of container. One-third cup dough patted into 4-inch disc yields 5-inch cookie. (Measure amount of dough used and diameter of cookie before and after baking. Make adjustments before making remaining cookies.)

3. Place cookies on *ungreased* baking sheet. Bake 10 minutes or until lightly browned. Remove with spatula to wire racks; cool completely.

4. Place chocolate in small resealable plastic freezer bag; seal bag. Microwave at MEDIUM (50% power) 1 minute. Turn bag over; microwave at MEDIUM 1 minute or until melted. Knead bag until chocolate is smooth.

5. Cut off very tiny corner of bag; pipe chocolate decoratively onto cookies. Let stand until chocolate is set.

6. Stack cookies between layers of waxed paper in container. Store loosely covered at room temperature up to 1 week.

Makes 9 (5-inch) cookies

Prefab Gingerbread House, continued

6. Bake cookies 8 minutes or until no indentation remains when touched in center. Immediately place cardboard patterns lightly on cookies; trim edges with sharp knife; discard trimmings. Return cookies to oven.

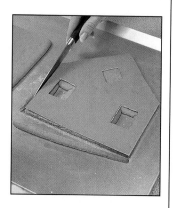

7. Bake 5 to 8 minutes or until cookies are very firm. Cool on pan 3 minutes. Remove cookies with large spatula to wire racks; cool completely. If cooled cookies remain moist in center, bake in 250°F oven 20 to 45 minutes. Do not burn. Cool completely on wire racks. Repeat with remaining dough and scraps.

8. To send cookies through the mail, wrap each gingerbread house cookie in bubble wrap to protect from moisture. Alternately stack cookies and bubble wrap beginning and ending with bubble wrap. Tape edges to hold stack together.

9. Package meringue powder and candies in airtight containers. Photocopy or handwrite recipe for Meringue Powder Royal Icing, directions for assembling house and decorating tips on decorative paper.

10. Pack cookies in sturdy box with plenty of packing peanuts, popped corn or paper around and between cookies and candies.

Makes 2 houses

Meringue Powder Royal Icing

¼ cup meringue powder
6 tablespoons water
1 box (16 ounces) powdered sugar, sifted

1. Beat meringue powder and water in medium bowl with electric mixer at low speed until well blended. Beat at high speed until stiff peaks form when beaters are lifted from mixture. (After beaters are lifted from mixture, stiff peaks should remain on top and when bowl is tilted, mixture will not slide around.)

2. Beat in sugar at low speed until well blended. Beat at high speed until icing is very stiff. Cover icing with damp cloth to prevent icing from drying.

Makes about 2½ cups

Note: Meringue Powder Royal Icing is used to glue the house together. It hardens after 5 minutes and completely dries in 20 to 30 minutes.

Directions For Assembling House

1. Prepare Meringue Powder Royal Icing. To make base of house, cover 12-inch-square piece of heavy cardboard with decorative paper.

2. Spoon icing into piping bag fitted with writing tip or resealable plastic freezer bag with one small corner cut off (line of icing squeezed out should measure ⅛ to ¼ inch thick). Pipe icing on edges of all pieces including bottom. Glue cookies together, 2 pieces at a time, at seams and onto base.

Prop house pieces into position with small jars or glasses until icing is set before gluing on additional pieces.

3. Glue assorted candies and decors onto house with icing. Let stand 1 hour or until set.

Decorating Tips: Glue rectangular candies, candy cane sticks, licorice or wafer cookies onto both sides of windows to make shutters. Glue pretzels, string licorice or candy cane sticks onto base of house to make fences. Stack gumdrops onto toothpicks or frost ice cream cones and decorate with sprinkles to make trees. Spread thin layer of icing onto roof and overlap pretzels, crackers, vanilla wafers, pastel or chocolate mints or marshmallows to make shingles. Glue peanut brittle, toffee or nuts onto side of house with icing to make chimney.

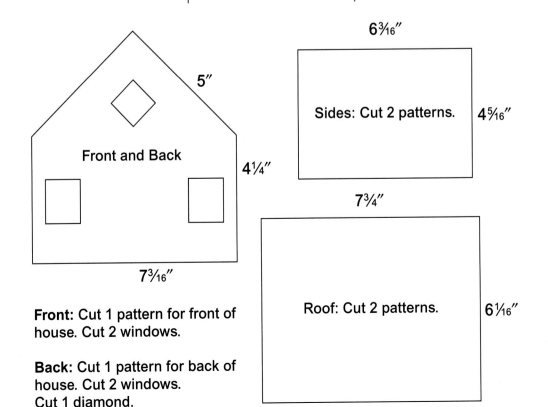

Front and Back

5″

4¼″

7³⁄₁₆″

Front: Cut 1 pattern for front of house. Cut 2 windows.

Back: Cut 1 pattern for back of house. Cut 2 windows. Cut 1 diamond.

6³⁄₁₆″

Sides: Cut 2 patterns.

4⁵⁄₁₆″

7¾″

Roof: Cut 2 patterns.

6¹⁄₁₆″

Canned Peanut Butter Candy Cookies

¾ **cup chunky peanut butter**

½ **cup butter or margarine, softened (page 74)**

1 **cup packed light brown sugar**

½ **teaspoon baking powder**

½ **teaspoon baking soda**

1 **egg**

1½ **teaspoons vanilla**

1¼ **cups all-purpose flour**

2 **cups quartered miniature peanut butter cups**

⅓ **cup milk chocolate chips or chopped milk chocolate bar**

EQUIPMENT: Decorative container

1. Beat peanut butter and butter in large bowl with electric mixer at medium speed until well blended. Beat in sugar, baking powder and baking soda until well blended. Beat in egg and vanilla until well blended. Beat in flour at low speed just until combined, scraping down side of bowl once. Stir in peanut butter cups with wooden spoon. Cover with plastic wrap. Refrigerate 1 hour or until firm.

2. Preheat oven to 375°F. For test cookie, measure inside diameter of container. Form ⅓ cup dough into ¼-inch-thick disc, about 2 inches in diameter less than the diameter of container. One-third cup dough patted into 4-inch disc yields 5-inch cookie. (Measure amount of dough used and diameter of cookie before and after baking. Make adjustments before making remaining cookies.)

3. Place cookies on *ungreased* baking sheet. Bake 10 minutes or until lightly browned. Remove with spatula to wire racks; cool completely.

4. Place chocolate in small resealable plastic freezer bag; seal bag. Microwave at MEDIUM (50% power) 1 minute. Turn bag over; microwave at MEDIUM 1 minute or until melted. Knead bag until chocolate is smooth.

5. Cut off very tiny corner of bag; pipe chocolate decoratively onto cookies. Let stand until chocolate is set.

6. Stack cookies between layers of waxed paper in container. Store loosely covered at room temperature up to 1 week.

Makes 9 (5-inch) cookies

Almond-Orange Shortbread

1 cup (4 ounces) sliced almonds, divided
1 orange
2 cups all-purpose flour
1 cup cold butter, cut into pieces
½ cup sugar
½ cup cornstarch
1 teaspoon almond extract

1. Preheat oven to 350°F. To toast almonds, spread ¾ cup almonds in single layer in large baking pan. Bake 6 minutes or until golden brown, stirring frequently. Remove almonds from oven. Cool completely in pan. *Reduce oven temperature to 325°F.*

2. Place almonds in work bowl of food processor. Process using on/off pulsing action until almonds are coarsely chopped.

3. Finely grate colored portion of orange peel using bell grater or hand-held grater. Measure 2 tablespoons orange peel.

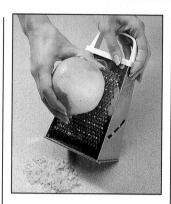

4. Add flour, butter, sugar, cornstarch, orange peel and almond extract to work bowl of food processor. Process using on/off pulsing action until mixture resembles coarse crumbs.

5. Press dough firmly and evenly into 10½×8½-inch rectangle on large *ungreased* baking sheet with fingers. Score dough into 1¼-inch squares with utility knife.

6. Press one slice of remaining almonds in center of each square.

7. Bake 30 to 40 minutes or until shortbread is firm when pressed and lightly browned.

8. Immediately cut into squares along score lines with sharp knife. Remove cookies with spatula to wire racks; cool completely.

9. Store loosely covered at room temperature up to 1 week.

Makes 5 dozen cookies

Lollipop Cookies

2 ounces
    unsweetened
    chocolate
3 cups all-purpose
    flour
1 teaspoon baking
    powder
1⅓ cups granulated
    sugar
1 cup butter,
    softened
    (page 74)
2 eggs
2 teaspoons vanilla
    Royal Icing
    (page 92)
    Decorator
    Frosting
    (page 16)
**EQUIPMENT AND
    DECORATIONS:**
    Craft sticks*
    Liquid or paste
        food coloring
    Toothpicks
    Assorted decors
        (optional)

*Available where cake decorating supplies are sold.

1. Preheat oven to 350°F. Place chocolate on cutting board; shave into small pieces with paring knife.

2. Melt chocolate in heavy, small saucepan over low heat, stirring constantly with wooden spoon until smooth. Set aside.

3. Combine flour and baking powder in small bowl with wooden spoon until well blended. Beat sugar and butter in large bowl with electric mixer at medium speed until light and fluffy, scraping down side of bowl once. Beat in eggs and vanilla until well blended. Gradually add flour mixture. Beat at low speed until blended, scraping down side of bowl once.

4. Remove half of dough from bowl; form into disc with lightly floured hands. Wrap disc in plastic wrap; refrigerate while working with remaining half of dough. Add chocolate to remaining dough in bowl. Beat at low speed until well blended.

5. Place chocolate dough on lightly floured surface; press into 6-inch square with lightly floured hands. Cut lengthwise into 4 equal strips with utility knife. Cut crosswise into 4 equal strips to form 16 squares.

6. Roll each square into ball. Place balls 3 inches apart on *ungreased* baking sheets. Place craft stick under each ball.

7. Press balls into 2½-inch circles using lightly floured bottom of drinking glass.

continued on page 92